HERBERT L. CLARKE
ELEMENTARY STUDIES

FOR
TRUMPET

Containing instructive text together with thirty progressive lessons and one hundred and sixteen exercises carefully graded and annotated.

Published in 2019 by Allegro Editions

Elementary Studies for Trumpet
ISBN: 978-1-9748-9984-5 (paperback)

Cover design by Kaitlyn Whitaker

Cover image: "Music Sheet" by Danielo,
courtesy of Shutterstock;
"Trumpet on White Background" by Walter Bilotta,
courtesy of Shutterstock

ALLEGRO EDITIONS

Introduction

During my career as a cornetist, I have given many thousand lessons to cornet players, from beginners to the best players in the country. Many cornet methods, all good, useful and highly recommended by me are available, but in this work I have had the beginner in mind. It is my purpose to help him lay a solid foundation by means of simple exercises, easy to play, without strain of any kind, and in this way assist him to reach the highest mark of perfection for which we are all striving.

If practiced in the proper way at the start, correct cornet playing is no more of an effort than ordinary deep breathing. To form the lips for producing a pure tone, to train the muscles of the face gradually without noticeable fatigue, to acquire endurance — all of which must be attained before one can become a successful cornet player — is the object of this series.

Many of the published methods do not treat sufficiently of the very beginning for those who have never produced the first tone upon a wind instrument, consequently I undertook to write a series of exercises in simplest form which will neither fatigue nor strain the student. Their further purpose is to gradually build up the strength of the facial muscles, to purify the tone without causing the usual weariness so common to most beginners, and finally to acquaint them with a knowledge of those fundamental principles most necessary for cornet study.

In the first place the Cornet is not such a difficult instrument to master as is supposed, if one commences in the *proper way* at the start. In more recent years obstacles have been overcome with ease that seemed impossible at the time the instrument was introduced. Manufacturers throughout the world have employed experts whose experiments have extended the range of the instrument, improved the intonation and perfected the mechanism, making possible the playing of music written for the voice, or for the Flute, Oboe, Clarinet or Violin, although the compass of the latter is beyond that of the Cornet.

This elementary work is divided into lessons, graduated so as to build up the *"embouchure"* without physical strain on the student. *"Embouchure"* is a term applied to the formation of the lips covered by the mouthpiece, the vibration necessary to produce the tone, and the training of the muscles of the face used in contracting the lips for a high note and relaxing them for a low note.

Hints

Here are a few *hints*, not rules, that years of experience in my professional work have taught me, which if followed out will enable the student to build up the *"embouchure"* without any noticeable strain.

"Always try to produce a musical tone from the very start." Even if it requires time to perfect this, *exert patience.*

"Always play softly, never harshly." Remember that the softer one plays when practicing the stronger the "embouchure" becomes, enabling the player to endure more than with the old way of resorting to brute force, which in a short time will destroy the nerves of the lips, the lips becoming numb.

"Always remember when the least fatigue is noticeable to rest a few moments, even if in the first few minutes of practice." To play a moment after the muscles are tired will place the student back even after weeks of work. A piece of string wound tightly around the finger produces numbness. To press the mouthpiece constantly against the lips produces the same effect upon the lips, which is harmful. Bear this illustration in mind and you will improve gradually and save your lips from breaking down.

"Never hold the lips rigid, but keep them soft and pliable, using only enough pressure to keep the mouthpiece firmly against the lips without the least air escaping outside the mouthpiece."

"Many students want to play solos after taking a few lessons when they know they are undertaking an impossibility. This is like the would-be athlete trying to run a hundred-yard dash in ten seconds without preparing himself beforehand by training. As an illustration, "Don't try to run five miles at the rate of a hundred yards in ten seconds."

Position of the Mouthpiece on the Lips

Take the Cornet in the left hand, grasping the valves gently, the instrument seemingly resting on the hand, which balances the Cornet properly. The first three fingers of the right hand are placed over the keys. Hold the Cornet in a horizontal position.

Place the mouthpiece in the middle of the lips in the easiest and most natural position so the two lips will vibrate equally in the center of the mouthpiece; neither two-third on the upper and one-third on the lower, nor one third on the upper and two-thirds on the lower, but *in the center*. In time this will produce an even tone with volume throughout the entire scale.

There are several positions advocated in cornet methods that contradict one another, but I have always found the easiest and most natural way the best for all.

Always keep the Cornet in a horizontal position, neither pointing up nor down. Should a player's upper jaw protrude, throw the head backward a little, and if the lower jaw protrudes, lower the head.

There is nothing more disagreeable looking than a soloist standing before an audience, pointing the instrument at the footlights instead of straight in front of him. The proper position should be acquired in the very first practice. Stand before a looking-glass to get the proper position and you will "see yourself as others see you." The looking-glass is an excellent "fault finder."

Commencing the Tone

When the mouthpiece is placed in the proper position on the lips, then pronounce the syllable "tu", softly at first. The tongue should be placed at the base of the upper teeth, naturally, and as this syllable is pronounced it performs a backward movement resembling the action of a valve.

This pronunciation determines the striking of the sound. Practice it easily, never in a rigid condition, and the tone will come clearer. Never allow the tongue to come between the teeth, because it is impossible to articulate distinctly or rapidly in this manner and the syllable "tu" cannot be pronounced with the tongue in this position. If you try to produce this sound with your tongue between your teeth, instead of at the base of the upper teeth, you will find a sound similar to "thu", which is wrong.

Method of Breathing
"Common sense teaches us more than all else"

Without air or wind there is no tone. Always commence a tone with the lungs inflated, or properly filled, and utilize all the air before inhaling again. Your lips may be perfect, your tongue in the proper position, but no tone can be produced without wind, any more than a locomotive, built perfectly in every way, can expect to move without steam.

Be careful to breathe regularly, inhale with freedom and exhale or blow carefully, never forcing the tone, but producing it naturally. In time you will realize that developing your chest, equalizing your power or generating it, are important factors and that the lips alone do not play the Cornet but only act as the vocal chords in the throat of a singer, which if strained will ruin the success of any vocalist.

Never abuse the lips by straining or pressing them and they will last a lifetime, growing stronger instead of weaker as the hours pass in diligent practice.

"Well begun is half done"

Music, One of the Great Arts

Melody is a tone picture, and for the guidance of the performer marks of expression are introduced by signs and words, placed over or under the notes or phrases to lend assistance in interpreting the composition in a musical style.

A picture is commenced by sketching the outline, which in its crude state is not always beautiful. So notes printed on the staff are simply an outline which requires certain markings to complete the work. As the colors are painted and blended the picture becomes more beautiful; in the same way the melody when played in accordance with the expression marks becomes more pleasant to hear.

These marks of expression are usually adapted from the Italian, and when used in connection with music are abbreviated, syllables, letters and signs being employed. Italian terms are also used to determine the time or tempo in which the music should be played. Here is a list of the terms and abbreviations most commonly used.

Allegretto *(all^{tto})* - moderately fast.
Allegro *(all^o)* - lively or fast.
Accelerando *(accel.)* - increasing in speed.
Andante *(and^{te})* - a moderately slow movement.
Adagio *(adg^o)* - a slow movement.
A tempo *(a t.)* - return to the original tempo.
Crescendo *(cresc.)* - increasing in loudness.
Diminuendo *(dim.)* - diminishing in loudness.
Forte *(f)* - loud.
Fortissimo *(ff)* - very loud.
Maestoso *(maest^o)* - with majesty or dignity.
Mezzo forte *(mf)* - half-loud.
Moderato *(mod^{to})* - at a moderate rate of speed.
Piano *(p)* - soft.
Pianissimo *(pp)* - very soft.
Rallentando *(rall.)* - growing slower and slower.
Ritardando *(ritard.* or *rit.)* - growing slower and slower.
A dot or dash (. ʼ) placed over or under a note indicates that it is to be played *staccato*, that is detached or short.
Sforzando *(sfz* or >) - to be performed with special stress or sudden emphasis.
Swell ======= a *crescendo* ===== and *decrescendo* =====

FIRST LESSON

In commencing this lesson be careful to read the Introduction through thoughtfully, referring to the different explanations when you are in doubt. Starting in the right way at the beginning will save years of hard work. Remember that cornet playing is as easy as breathing, except when playing solos or in marching bands, etc., which takes more effort.

These first exercises are written in the simplest form, the intervals are close and melodies are kept in the middle register. Play each exercise through many times in strict time without a mistake until it becomes easy and is thoroughly mastered.

In order that the student may keep perfect time I have arranged a lower part in duet form for the teacher. In my own experience this has been of great benefit to the pupil.

I would also advise the pupil to use a Metronome, an instrument with a short pendulum and a sliding weight, which when set in motion by clockwork serves to measure the time in music.

Notes in music are divided as follows, whole, half, quarter, eighth, sixteenth, etc. The first three lessons contain whole notes, which are shaped like a zero (o). Each whole note receives four equal counts and is the equivalent of four quarter notes. This constitutes one measure of time, called common time, and is marked at the beginning of every piece of music after the "clef sign" (ϕ), sometimes as 4/4 or "C", thus:

The fingering is marked below each note until the student becomes familiar with it; also the letters or names of the notes are placed above them. "O" represents open tone, use no fingers. "1", first finger, "2", second finger and "3", third finger. Place the tips of the fingers on the top of the pistons and always keep them there.

Pronounce the syllable "tu" in a firm manner, never push a tone or puff the cheeks out. Play each exercise over hundreds of times, in the same way a person would do calisthenic exercises, each motion repeated many times to strengthen certain muscles of the body. Practice in the same way on the Cornet, and the strength of the lips will be gradually built up.

Count; 1, 2, 3, 4, for each measure in strict time.

All the exercises have been provided with Metronome marks in order to guide the student as to proper tempo.

Some beginners in starting their first tone, find "G" easier: others "C"

Practice on the tone that is easier for you. Continue on the same note until a clear tone is produced.

…ould "G" be the easier, follow the above instructions; then relax the lips, blow softer, until "C" can be produced in the same manner, before starting on the first exercise.

Directions for exact speed of tempo according to a Metronome: Place the pendulum weight at the figure given in brackets: for example in Ex. 1, when the pendulum weight is placed at 60, each tick is equal to a *quarter* note.

Count 1 2 3 4 Met. (♩ = 60)

1

Student

Teacher

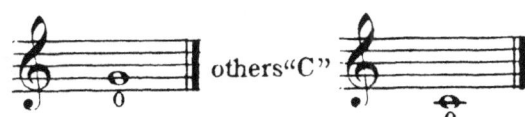

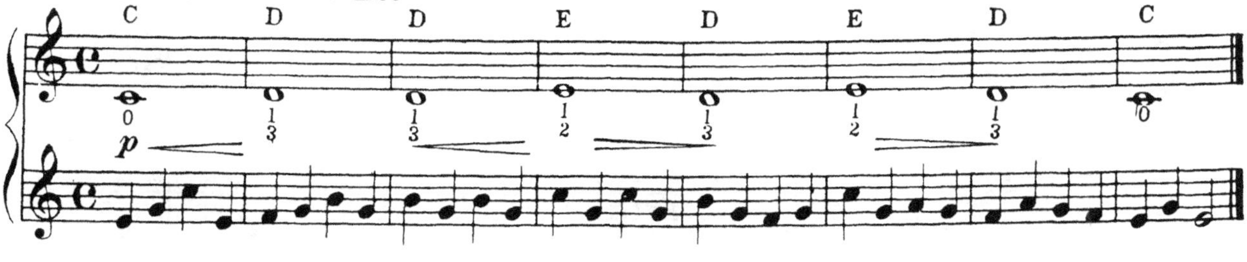

2

Met. (♩ = 80)

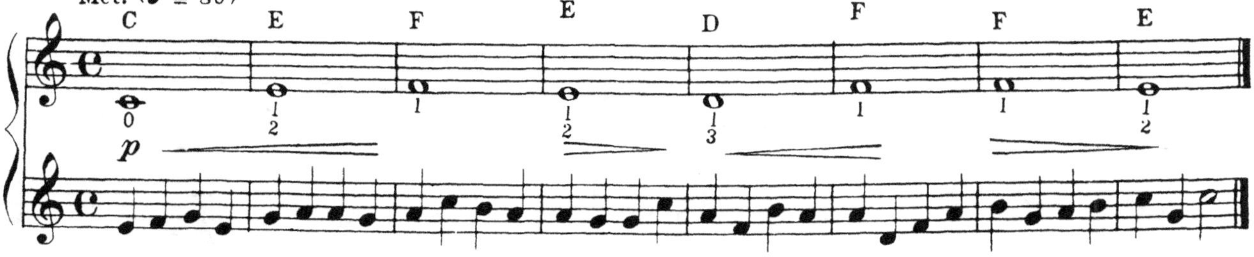

3

Met. (♩ = 80)

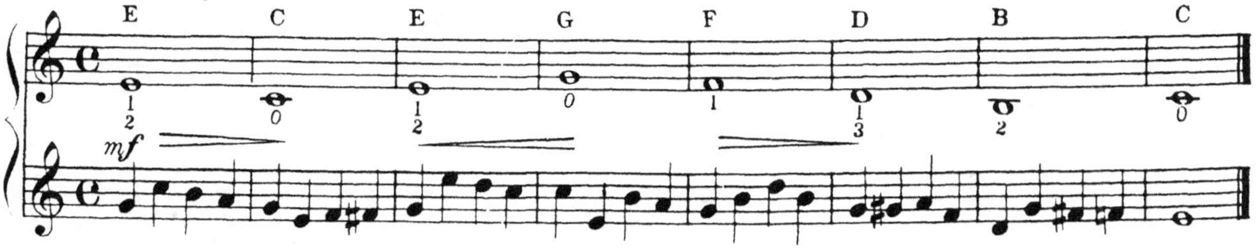

4

Met. (♩ = 80)

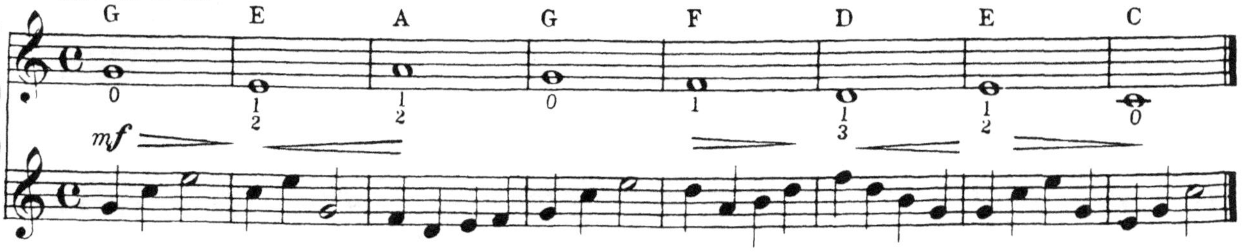

5

Met. (♩ = 92)

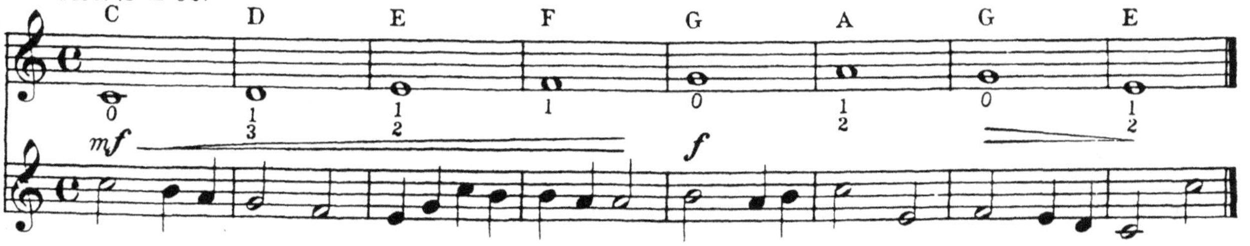

SECOND LESSON

A continuation of easy studies, arranged in duet form, but ascending a step or two as the lips grow stronger, to a full octave.

Do not practice after the lips feel tired or refuse to vibrate. Rest a few moments, then try again. *Use patience always.*

THIRD LESSON

In this lesson the duets are dispensed with, as by this time the student should have a correct idea of "tempo" or "time" and will be able to count alone by marking the time with his foot, or by using the Metronome and setting it at the time marked at the beginning of each exercise, thus: ♩=100 - when the pendulum weight is placed at 100, each tick is equal to a quarter-note.

The following exercises are twice the length of the first ten.

FOURTH LESSON

In the previous lessons only whole notes were used—now divide them. A *whole note* requires *four beats*, consequently a *half note* requires *two beats* and *two half notes* equal *one whole note*.

A half note is shaped like a zero, but with a stem, ♩

Always take a full breath before beginning to play. Notice that commas (ʼ) are placed above the staff at certain intervals; they are used in all the exercises to show when to breathe.

FIFTH LESSON

By this time the student must have become familiar with the notes and their names with the fingering. He must have formed a general idea of the change of pressure, contracting the lips for a higher note, with more power from the chest and relaxing the lips for a lower note, with less wind power.

This lesson treats of *whole* and *half* notes.

SIXTH LESSON

There have been exercises in *whole* and *half* notes, now the *quarter notes* will be introduced. Each *quarter note* receives one beat in 4/4 or common time.

Two quarter notes equal a *half* note, and *four quarter* notes equal a *whole* note.

A *quarter* note is a round dot with a stem, ♩

Try and play four measures in one breath, practicing endurance.

SEVENTH LESSON

This lesson contains exercises made up as a general review, as far as the student has progressed, using *whole, half* and *quarter* notes.

Give full value for every note, remembering to count **1-2-3-4** for a *whole* note; **1-2** for a *half* note, and **1**, for a *quarter* note.

EIGHTH LESSON

The Seventh Lesson taught the use of *whole, half* and *quarter* notes. There is still another form of notation; by placing a *dot* after any note, its time value is prolonged by one-half. For example; a *dot* written after a *half-note*, thus: 𝅗𝅥· gives this note the time value of *three quarter notes*.

By practicing faithfully all the peceding exercises the student will have strengthened his lips sufficiently to add two more notes to the scale above C in the third space, and three notes below C on the first line below the staff.

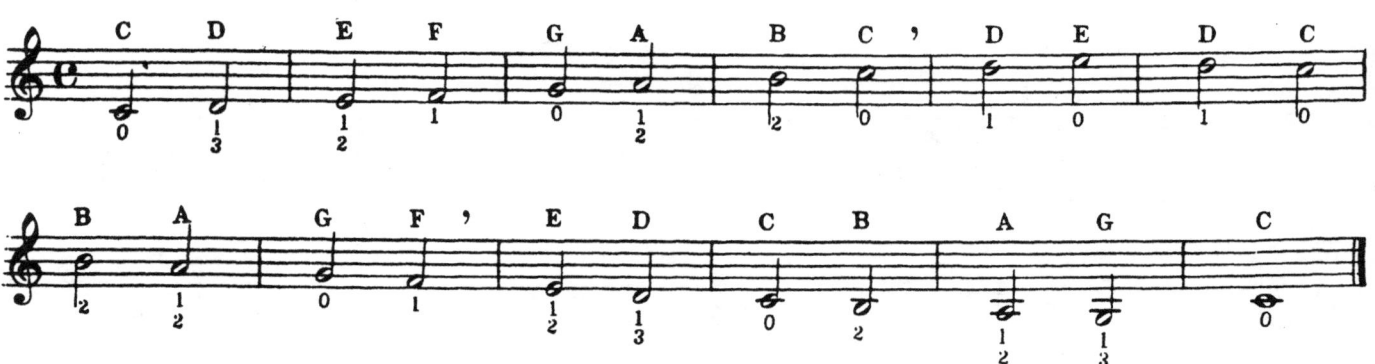

Memorize this example thoroughly before commencing the following exercises.
Lines above or below the staff are called *leger* or *added* lines.

NINTH LESSON

Never change the position of the mouthpiece on the lips, nor hold the lips too rigid. When playing intervals or "skips" contract the lips for high notes and relax them for lower notes. This strengthens the muscles of the face without causing cramps.

Always keep the lips moist, wet them with the tongue because they will vibrate easier, and in time respond to the least wind from the chest, saving power. It is wrong to wipe the lips or play with dry lips.

This lesson is a continuation of the preceding one, except that greater intervals are used. This will make the *"embouchure"* more flexible and enable the student to gain greater control of the tone as well as the pitch of the notes.

The next exercise should be played in a bold manner, striking each tone firmly and with more power, taking care to give each note equal force.

Octaves are difficult to play on the Cornet. In Exercise No. **45** play much slower, striking each tone firmly and boldly.

TENTH LESSON

This lesson is comprised of exercises of longer duration which gives the student an opportunity to gain facility in reading music and enables him to become familiar with intervals, thereby contributing to his gradual improvement and ultimate perfection.

Never practice a moment after the lips seem fatigued. Rest a few minutes, then begin once more.

Notice the breathing spaces, eight measures to one breath.

ELEVENTH LESSON

In these exercises a few marks of expression, explained in the introductory remarks, are used.

Exert patience for the longer intervals of breathing. This endurance is of the greatest importance for future work. It trains the will power, which is the secret of high notes.

TWELFTH LESSON

Common time (**C** or $\frac{4}{4}$), sometimes called four-four time, contains *four quarter notes* in a measure.

Two-four time ($\frac{2}{4}$) contains *two quarter notes* in a measure, and will be taken up in this lesson. Two additional tones of the scale, (F and G), are also introduced.

To play these notes properly the lips are compressed still more, and more power from the chest is needed.

A *dot* placed after a quarter note increases the value one-half; viz ($\sigma\cdot$) equals one and one-half beats. An *eighth note* is half the value of a *quarter note*, and is given half a beat. It is written the same as a quarter note, but has a tail at the end of the stem: ($\flat$).

To simplify the reading of music, groups of eighth notes are written (♫ ♫ or ♬) instead of (♪ ♪ ♪ ♪).

Dividing the time for eighth notes, in two four $\frac{2}{4}$ *time;*

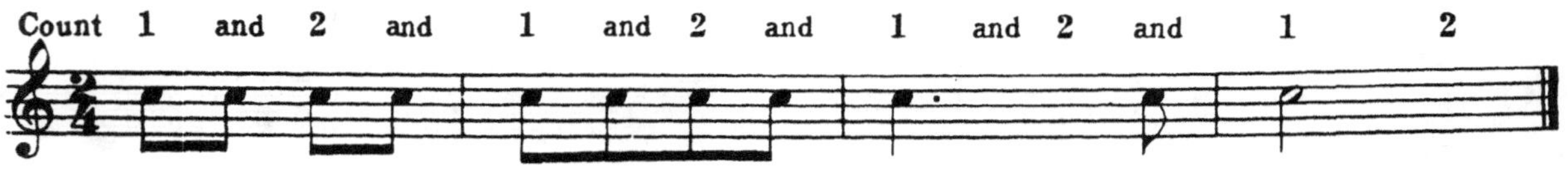

THIRTEENTH LESSON

There are *rests,* or *silent beats,* which correspond exactly with the value of the note, that is *whole, half, quarter, eighth,* etc.

Example

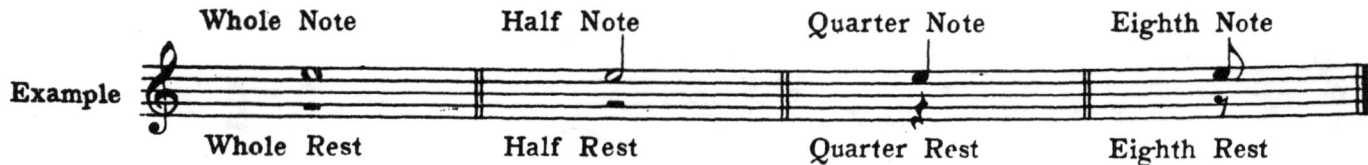

Signs are employed to avoid writing the same music twice, they are called *repeats, Dal Segnos, Da Capos* and may be used for one measure, one strain, or back to the beginning.

Example

61

62

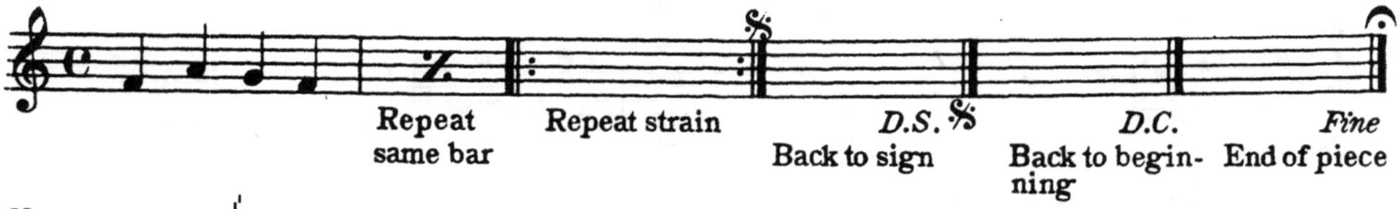

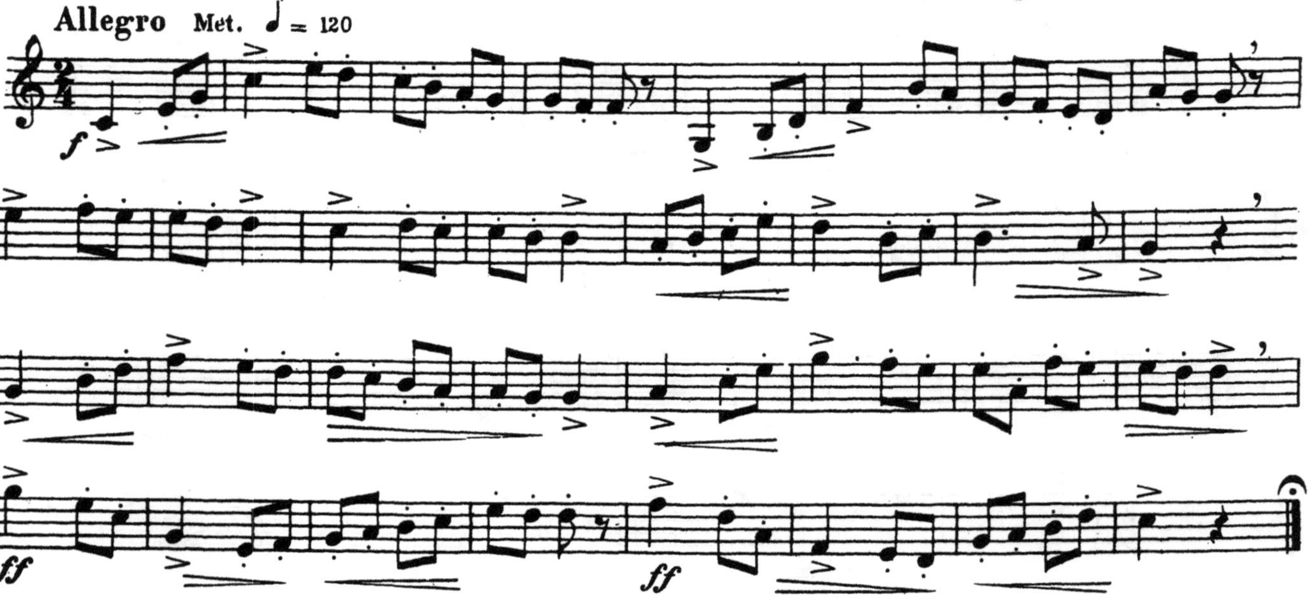

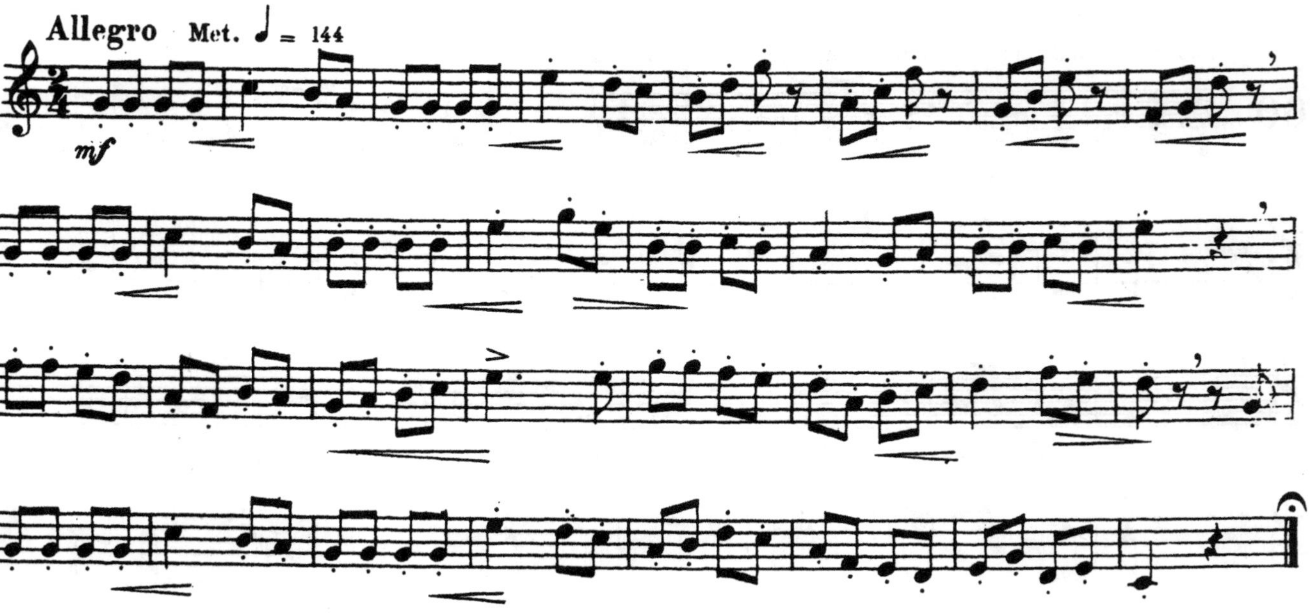

FOURTEENTH LESSON

The previous lessons treated only of the *Diatonic scale* in C. There are thirteen *Major keys* or *scales*, all formed in the same manner as the *scale* or *key* of C. The *Chromatic scale*, composed of *semi* or *half tones* is now introduced.

A *sharp* (♯) raises the note a half tone. A *flat* (♭) lowers the note a half tone. A *natural* (♮) signifies a return to the original tone. In ascending the scale *sharps* are used; in descending *flats* are used.

The Chromatic Scale

Memorize this *Chromatic scale* **THOROUGHLY**, before proceeding.

A *pause* is marked thus ⌢ or ⌣ : which means, when placed over or under a note, that the tone must be sustained. When placed over or under a rest, silence must be prolonged. And when placed over a Double Bar: ‖ , means the conclusion of the piece.

To build a Major Diatonic scale, observe the following rules.

The *key of "C" Major*, is the *model* of all *Major keys*.

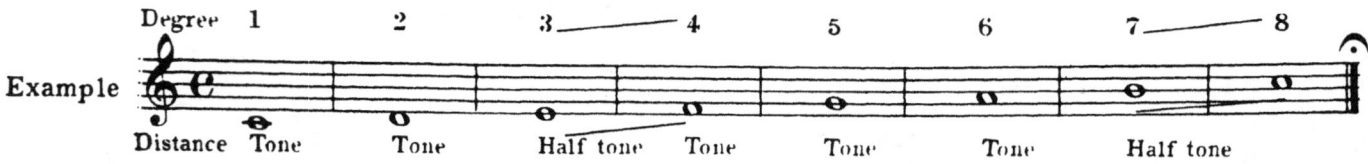

In all Major keys the half-tones occur between 3 and 4, and 7 and 8. All other intervals are whole tones; making *five whole tones* and *two half tones*.

There are thirteen Major keys; each derives its name from a certain number of *sharps* or *flats* placed immediately after the *clef* 𝄞; this is known as the *signature*.

FIFTEENTH LESSON

Sharps (♯), flats (♭) and naturals (♮) not found in the *signature* but set before a note in the midst of a composition, are called *accidentals*.

When a note, that is raised (♯) or lowered (♭) occurs more than once in the same measure, it is unnecessary to use the accidental again.

Example

This is one of the *most important rules* in *music*, and *must be remembered!*

Another sign will be employed, called the *slur:* ⌒ When written over or under a *group of notes*, shows that they must be played smoothly, sustaining the tone, using the *tongue* to *start* the phrase *only*.

Example

This same sign is also used to connect notes of the same degree, it is then called a *tie*. When two notes are *tied* the second note is not repeated, it is merely held for the duration of the time value.

Thus:

Never take breath when a slur is used!

Before closing this lesson, there are two new subjects to be explained. A new *time* or *tempo;* and a *new key.*
In *Common Time*, or $\frac{4}{4}$, there are *four beats* to the measure. In $\frac{2}{4}$ *time, two beats*. Now take $\frac{3}{4}$ *time*, with *three beats* to the measure, which contains *three quarter notes*.

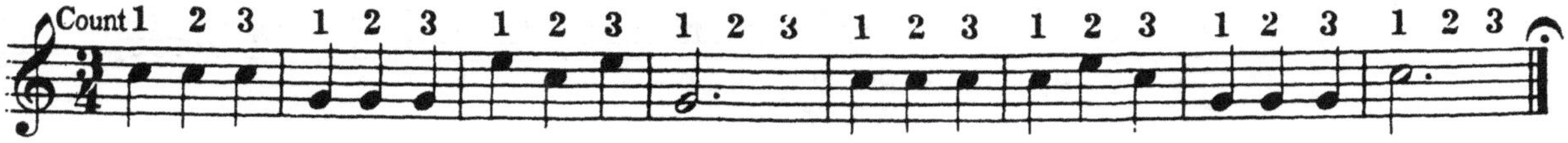

The key of "F" is known by its *signature* of *one flat*, placed on the *third line* of the *staff*, (immediately following the *clef sign*) which is "B♭", and this *key* is built exactly like the *key* of "C" which is explained in the *Fourteenth Lesson*, using the same *degrees*, and following the same *rules*. From 3 to 4, a half tone, also from 7 to 8.

To attract the attention of the student, the notes to be changed in the different keys, will be enclosed in brackets.

Key of F

Signature One Flat

Example

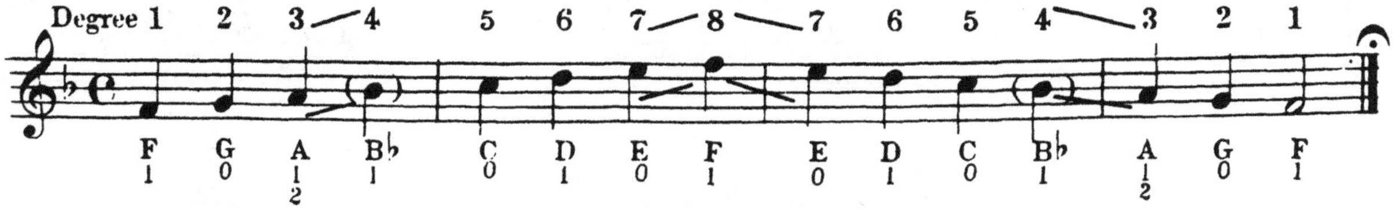

69

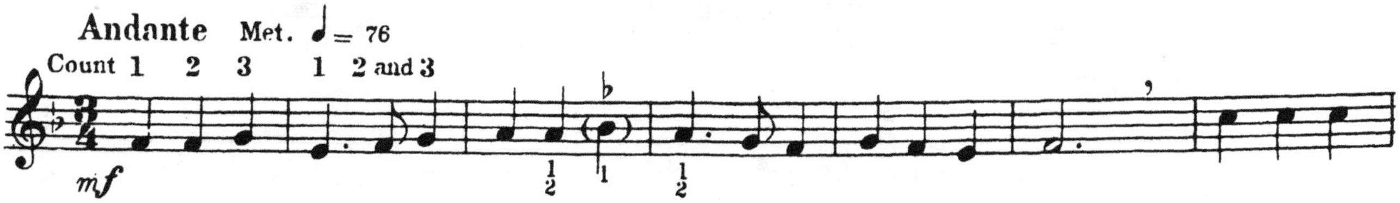

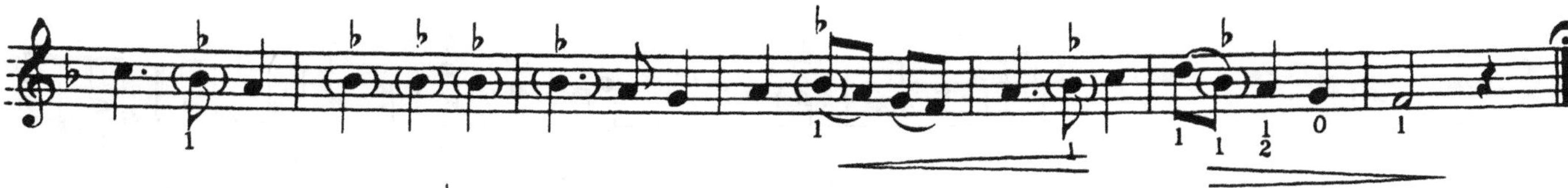

70

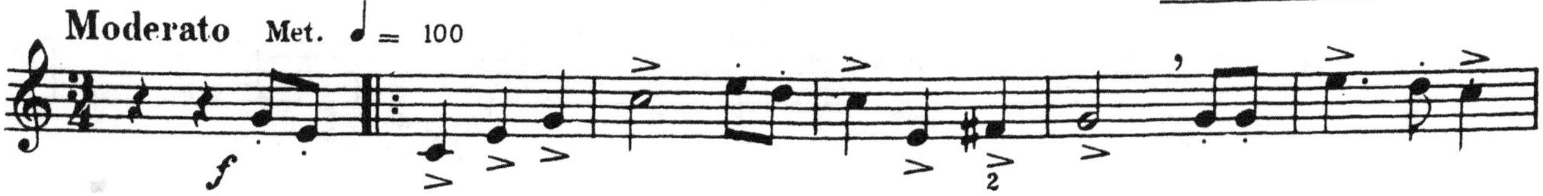

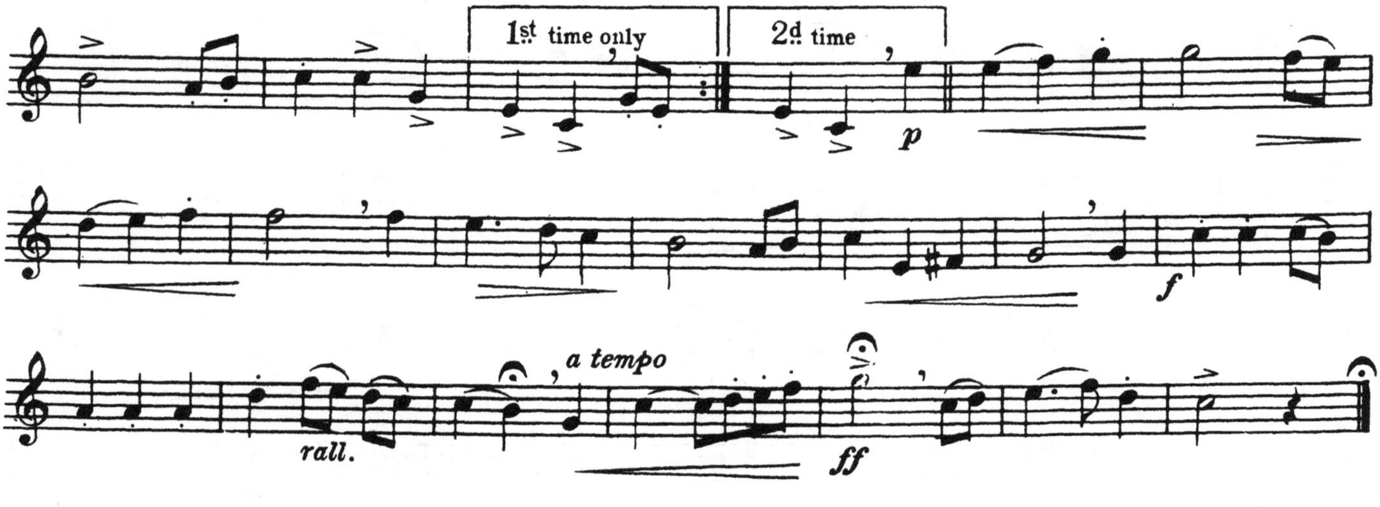

SIXTEENTH LESSON

SEVENTEENTH LESSON

Another form of notation is the *sixteenth note*, (♬) which is half the value of the *eighth note*, (♪) and is written with *two tails* to the stem. There are *four sixteenth notes* to *one quarter beat*.

Groups of *sixteenth* notes are connected by a double brace to simplify the reading of music.

The *sixteenth rest* also has two tails (𝄾) and when written denotes *one sixteenth* silence.

A *dot* written after an *eighth note* adds to the note one-half of its time value; one-half of one-eighth equals one-sixteenth. In musical notation this is written: ♪. ♬ or ♪. ♬ to one beat.

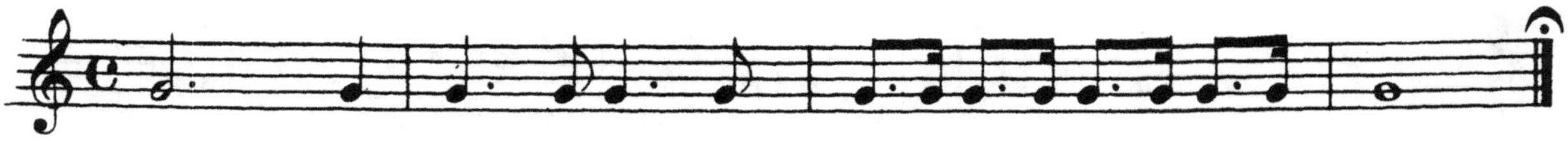

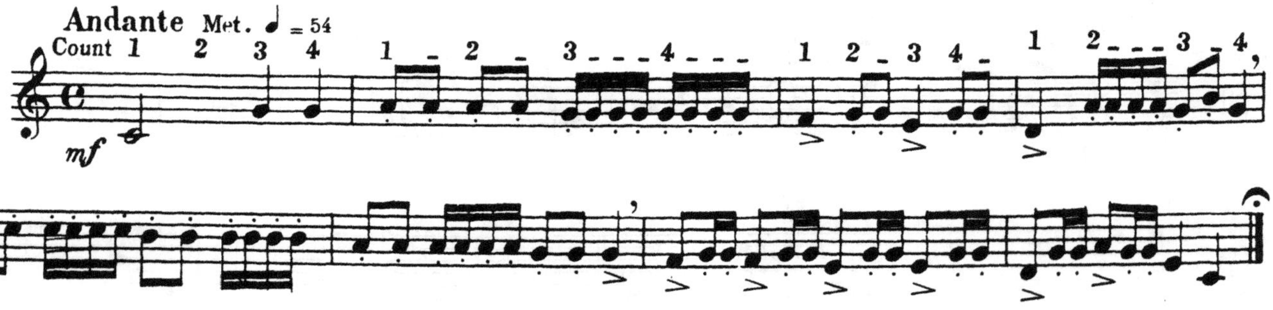

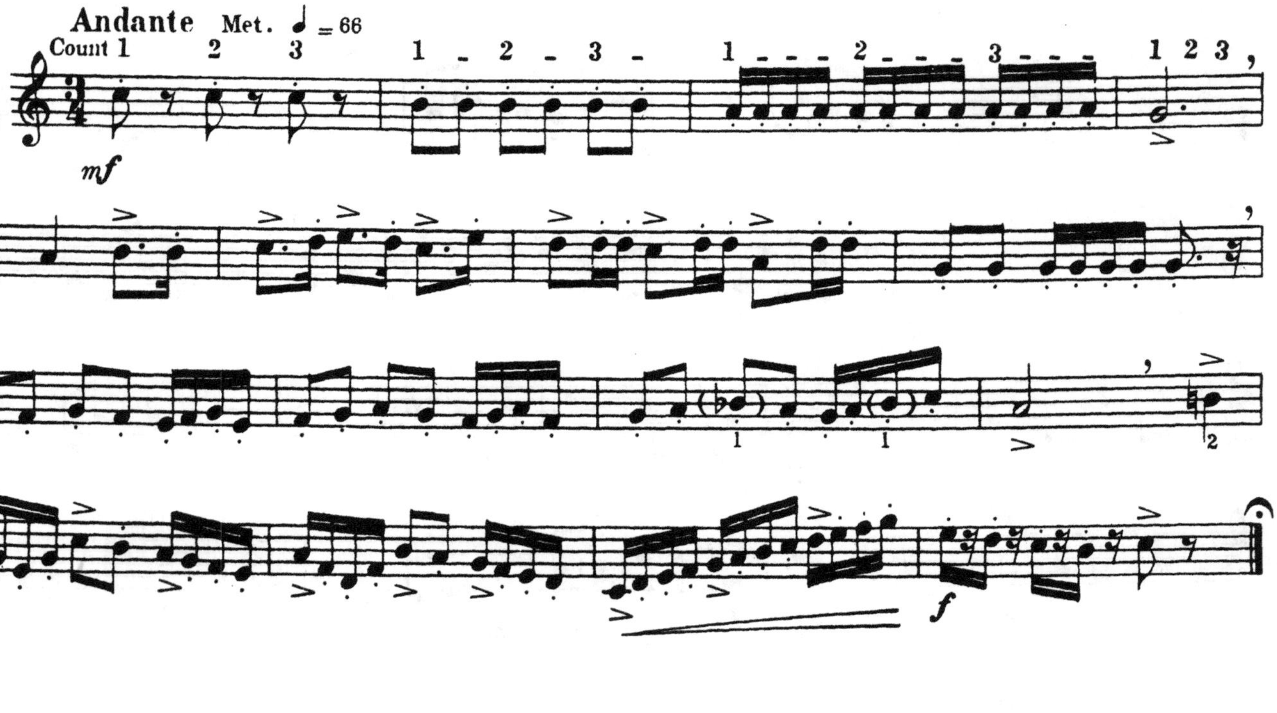

EIGHTEENTH LESSON

The *key of* "G" is known by its *signature* of *one sharp*, placed on the *fifth line* of the staff; (F♯) and is built by following the same rules as in the preceding keys.   From 3 to 4 and 7 to 8 half tones.

NINETEENTH LESSON

Still another division of time is a group of *three notes* called *triplets*. In counting *half time* or *Alla Breve* ¢, (♩♩♩) equals (♩♩): or in two-four time (♪♪♪) equals (♪♪) or (♪♪♪♪♪♪) equals (♪♪).

These *triplets* are also used in various ways; for instance a new time called *six-eighth* time 6/8 denoting six eighth notes in a measure and counting six beats in slow time and two beats in faster time.

There are four divisions of time using eighth notes: 3/8, 6/8, 9/8, 12/8 ; three beats, six beats, nine beats and twelve beats: or one, two, three and four beats in a measure.

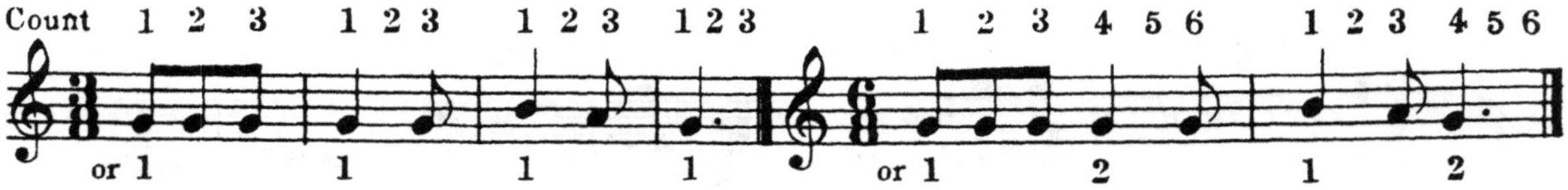

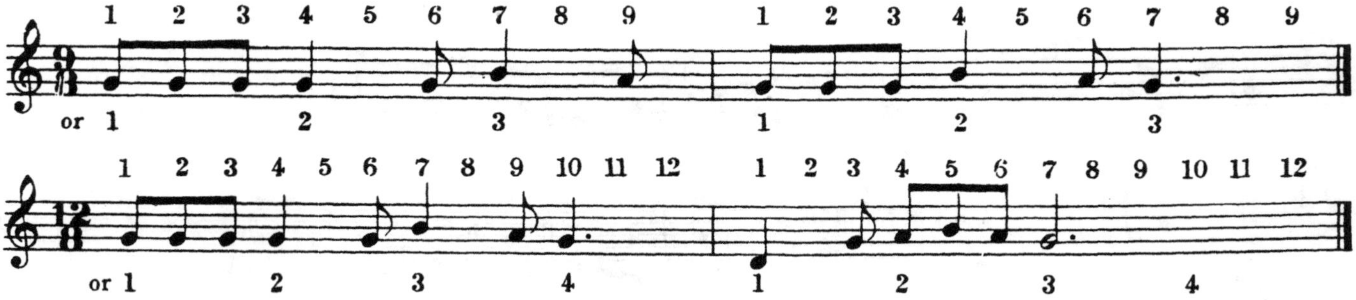

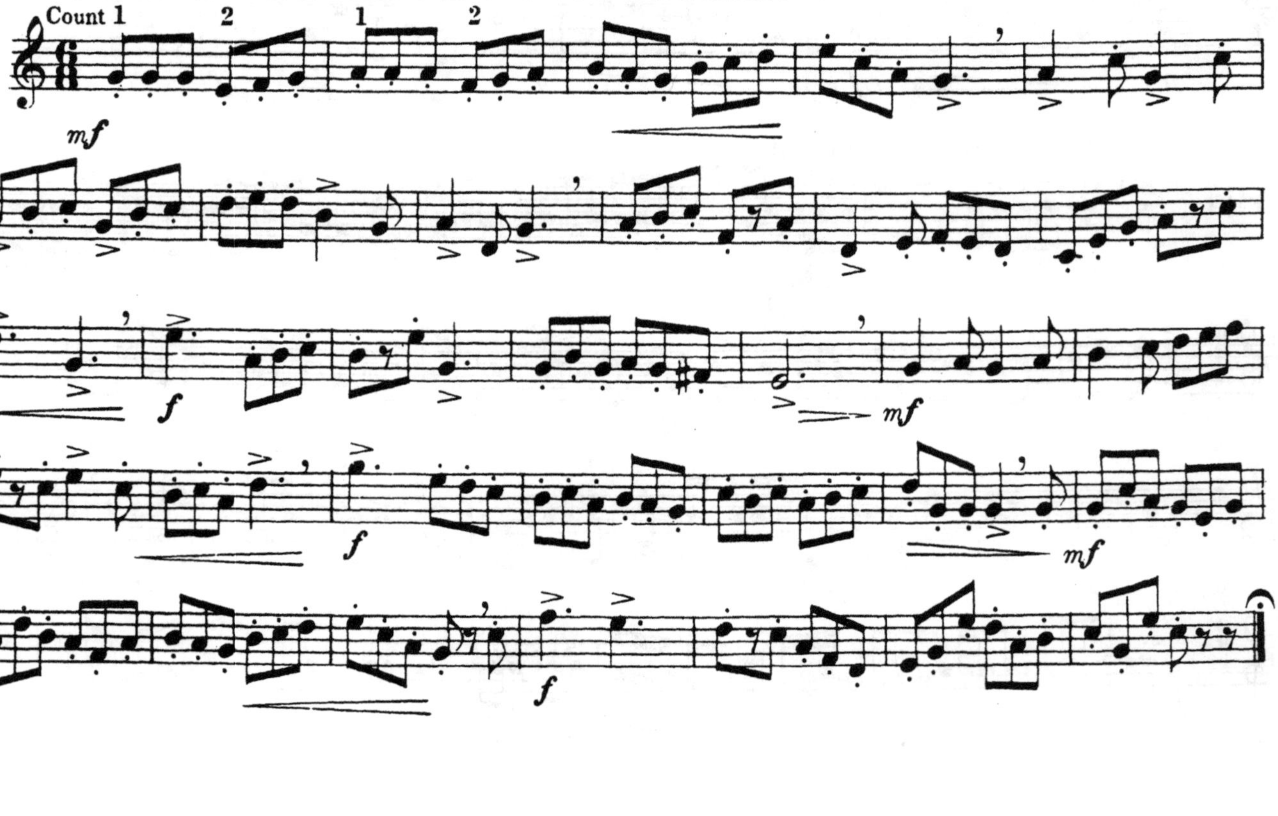

TWENTIETH LESSON

Syncopation or *syncopated time;* is sometimes called *broken time,* and is illustrated best in the following examples. When syncopated passages or phrases occur, the accent falls on the second note of the measure.

Example

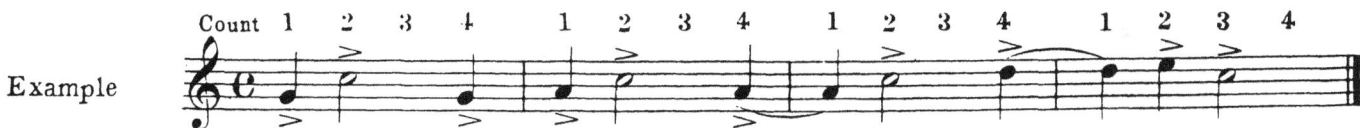

The tie is used, connecting the last note of the second measure to the first note in the third measure; to be sustained two beats.

These examples present *syncopation* as used in various tempi.

Example

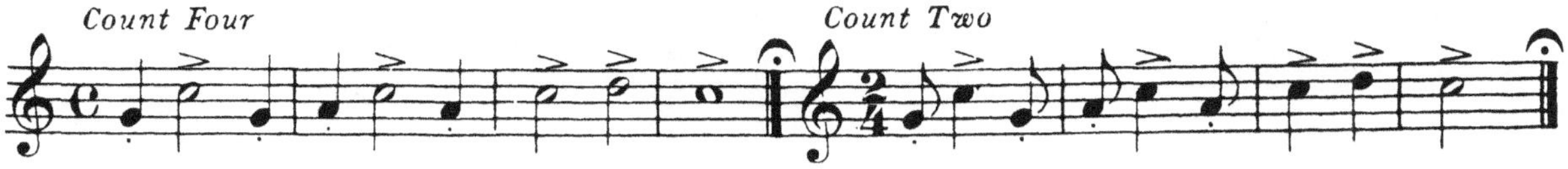

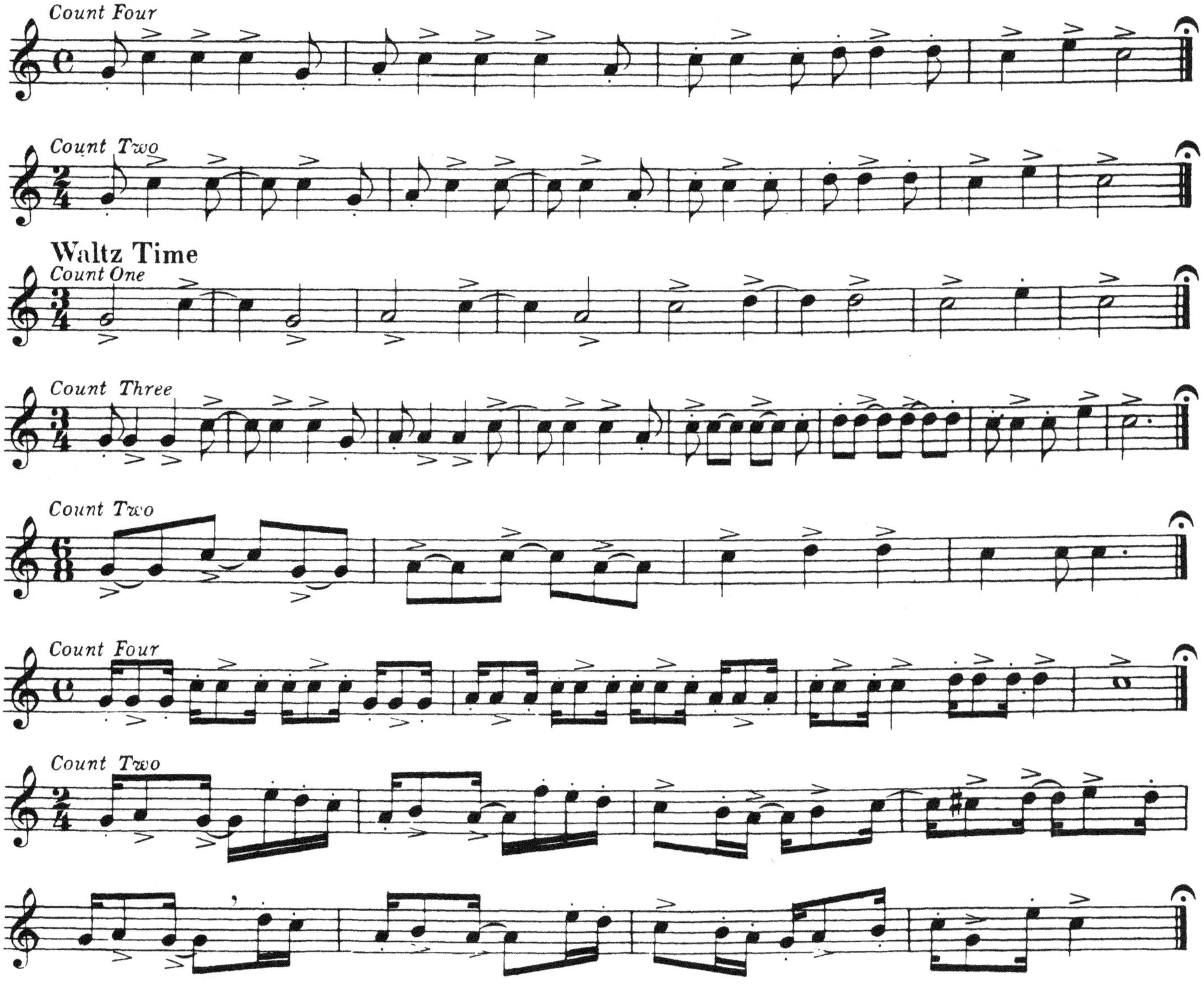

TWENTY-FIRST LESSON

The *key of* "B♭" is known by its *signature* of *two flats*, which are, "B♭" on the third line, and "E♭" in the fourth space.

TWENTY-SECOND LESSON

The *key of* "D" is known by its *signature* of *two sharps*, which are, "F#" on the fifth line, and "C#" in the third space.

TWENTY-THIRD LESSON

The *key of* "Eb" is known by its *signature* of *three flats*, which are, "Bb" on the third line, "Eb" in the fourth space, and "Ab" in the second space.

TWENTY-FOURTH LESSON

The *key of* "A" is known by its *signature* of *three sharps*, which are, "F#" on the fifth line, "C#" in the third space, and "G#" in the space above the staff.

TWENTY-FIFTH LESSON

The *key of* "A♭" is known by its *signature* of *four flats*, which are, "B♭" on the third line, "E♭" in the fourth space, "A♭" in the second space, and "D♭" on the fourth line.

TWENTY-SIXTH LESSON

The *key of* "E" is known by its *signature* of *four sharps*, which are, "F#" on the fifth line, "C#" in the third space, "G#" in the space above the staff, and "D#" on the fourth line.

TWENTY-SEVENTH LESSON

The *key of* "D♭" has *five flats*, which are, "B♭" on the third line, "E♭" in the fourth space, "A♭" in the second space, "D♭" on the fourth line and "G♭" on the second line.

TWENTY-EIGHTH LESSON

The *key of* "B" has *five sharps*, which are, "F#" on the fifth line, "C#" in the third space, "G#" in the space above the staff, "D#" on the fourth line and "A#" in the second space.

TWENTY-NINTH LESSON

The *key of* "G♭" has *six flats*, which are, "B♭" on the third line, "E♭" in the fourth space, "A♭" in the second space, "D♭" on the fourth line, "G♭" on the second line and "C♭" in the third space.

Key of G♭

Signature Six Flats

Example

113 Moderato Met. ♩ = 100

The *key of* "F♯" has *six sharps*, which are, "F♯" on the fifth line, "C♯" in the third space, "G♯" in the space above the staff, "D♯" on the fourth line, "A♯" in the second space, and "E♯" in the fourth space.

Key of F♯

Signature Six Sharps

Example

Notice: The *keys of* "G♭" and "F♯" both sound the same, and are fingered alike, but are written differently, and are two distinct keys.

This exercise is the same as No. 113, same fingering, sounds alike, but is written in the key of F♯
This sign (𝄪) is a *double sharp;* which means the note is raised *two half tones*.

THIRTIETH LESSON

After having finished with this series, the student should be sufficiently advanced to play music of medium difficulty, and I would advise everyone to join some amateur band or orchestra, in order to gain more experience.

For your own advancement, the last fifteen lessons should be reviewed thoroughly, playing every exercise exactly in time and with *perfect* tonal quality; without breaking on a single tone, and correcting each mistake by immediate repetition.

To be still more ambitious play each exercise at least ten times *consecutively* without a break of any kind.

DO NOT ALLOW AN EXERCISE TO BEAT YOU, OR GET THE BEST OF YOU AT ANY TIME!

DO NOT CHEAT YOURSELF!

Remember that *YOU* have the chance of becoming the most perfect Cornet player in the world!

There is published a Second Series of Cornet Studies, comprising 190 Exercises expressly for technic and endurance for the advanced player, and if the explanations in it are carefully adhered to, will enable the student to practice for hours, reach the highest notes above the staff with ease, also conquering the most difficult passages known for the Cornet.

No. 116 should be played *pp* throughout in a single breath, and repeated many times daily when beginning to practice.

STUDY

This study will be considered difficult. It calls for practical demonstration of all the experience gained in this work, should be played very slowly at first, and not practiced too long at a time.

EXAMPLES

These examples show the extended range of the Cornet, made possible through training the lips to be flexible and generating the power of the chest and diaphram.

This last example is my daily exercise, playing the three octaves of chromatics *four times* in one breath.

www.ingramcontent.com/pod-product-compliance
Lightning Source LLC
Chambersburg PA
CBHW081356040426
42451CB00017B/3471